Traditional Jam Recipes

by

Jane Romsey

This edition copyright © 2012 Jane Romsey.
All rights reserved.

Cover art copyright © 2012 Maz Scales http://www.artbymaz.com

Conversion Charts	8
Introduction	13
Section 1. Cakes	14
Victoria Sandwich Sponge Cake	14
Honey and Orange Tea Loaf	16
Cut and Come Again Cake	17
Rock Cakes or Buns	18
Moist Lemon Cake	19
Raspberry Buns	21
Paradise Cake	22
Marmalade Cake	24
Oatmeal Gingerbread	25
Marmalade and Ginger Slice	26
Traditional British Christmas Cake	28
Battenberg Cake	31
British Fairy Cakes	33
Never-Fail Boiled Fruit Cake	34

Parkin	**36**
Tantallon Cakes	**38**
Madeira Cake	**40**
Tea Fruit Cake	**41**
Seed Cake	**42**
Eccles Cakes	**44**
Section 2. Puddings	**46**
Very Proper English Custard	**47**
Spotted Dick	**49**
Bakewell Pudding	**51**
Treacle Tart	**52**
Apple Crumble	**53**
Jam Roly-Poly	**54**
Manchester Tart	**56**
British Sticky Toffee Pudding	**58**
Chocolate Fudge Pudding	**60**
Traditional English Sherry Trifle	**62**

Bread Pudding	64
Glastonbury Pudding	66
Bread and Butter Pudding	68
Figgy Pudding	70
Marmalade Pudding	72
Belvoir House Pudding	74
Ginger and Pear Upside-down Pudding	76
Traditional Rice Pudding	78
Chester Pudding	80
Steamed Syrup Sponge Pudding	81
Monmouth Pudding	84
Chocolate Bread and Butter Pudding	86
Section 3. Scones	88
Basic Plain Scones	90
Basic Tea Scones	91
Buttermilk Scones	93
Currant Scones	94

Treacle Scones	96
Apple Scones	97
Walnut and Raisin Scones	99
Cheese Scones	101
Potato Scones	102
Cheddar and Chive Scones	103
Soured Cream Scones	105
Strawberry Yoghurt Scones	107
Orange and Cherry Scones	109
Honey Scones	111
Dropped Scones	113
Section 4. Biscuits	114
Digestives	115
Gingernuts	116
Flapjacks	117
Shrewsbury Biscuits	118
Ayrshire Shortbread	120

Almond Shortbread	121
Petticoat Tails	122
Garibaldi Biscuits	123
Cornish Fairings	124
Abernethy Biscuits	126
Jam Thumb Biscuits	127
Bourbon Biscuits	129
Custard Creams	131
Anzac Biscuits	133
Treacle Bites	134
Rich Tea Biscuits	135
Savory Cheesy Biscuits	136
Coffee Biscuits	137
Arrowroot Biscuits	138
Jammie Dodgers	139
Crumpets	140

Conversion Charts

If you would prefer to use cup measurements I'm putting a conversion chart in here. I did not want to include the conversion in each recipe as it would make the ingredients lists very cluttered.

Weights vs. Measures
The most accurate way to bake is to weigh ingredients.
-Professional bakers weigh ingredients.
-In Europe, home bakers weigh ingredients.
-American home bakers measure.

Baking Measurements English and Metric
How to accurately measure dry ingredients.

Weighing ingredients is the most accurate method. If measuring with utensils, always use standard dry measurement cups and spoons.

Stir flour, powdered sugar, cocoa etc., until light and loose.
Sift first if recipe instructs to do so.
Use a tablespoon to lightly spoon into the cup until it is heaped up above the edge.
Don't shake or tap to settle flour.
Level off with the straightedge, not flat side of a spatula.

Remember: Each type of flour or ingredient will weigh a different amount per cup. Unless they are "standardized" measuring cups and spoons, they may vary depending on where they are bought.

Dry Measurement
Pinch = 1/16 teaspoon
Dash = 1/8 teaspoon or less
1 teaspoon = 1/3 tablespoon = 5 ml
3 teaspoons = 1 tablespoon = 15 ml
2 tablespoons = 1/8 cup or 1 ounce
4 tablespoons = 1/4 cup
5 tablespoons + 1 teaspoon = 1/3 cup
10 tablespoons + 2 teaspoons = 2/3 cup
8 tablespoons = 1/2 cup
1/2 cup + 2 tablespoons = 5/8 cup
12 tablespoons **OR** 1/2 c + 1/4 c = 3/4 cup
16 tablespoons = 1 cup
Zest of 1/2 lemon rind = 3/8 oz = 1 tablespoon
Zest of 1/4 orange rind = 3/8 oz = 1 tablespoon

Fluid Measurement
Measure liquids in a liquid measuring cup or beaker.
Set the cup or beaker on a flat surface.
Look at the amount at eye level.

1 cup = 8 fl.ounces = 237 ml
2 cups = 1 pint = 16 oz = 473 ml (0.473 liters)
4 cups = 2 pints = 1 qt = 32 fl. oz.= 946 ml (0.946 liters)
4 quarts = 1 gallon

oz. = ounce or ounces
c. = cup

T. = tbsp.= tablespoon
t. = tsp. = teaspoon
g = gram or grams = 0.035 oz lb. = pound = 454 grams
1 ounce = 28.35 grams
1 liter = 1.06 quarts

Ingredient Weight Equivalents
Stir, spoon and level method of measuring dry ingredients used.

Dry Ingredients
All-purpose flour 1 cup = 4 oz = 112g
Cake flour 1 cup = 3.75 oz = 105g
Bran, dry (not cereal) 1 cup = 2 oz = 56g
Bread flour 1 cup = 4.5 oz = 126g
Soy flour (defatted) 1 cup = 4 oz = 112g
Cornmeal 1 cup = 5.33 oz = 150g
Cocoa (baking) 1/4 cup = 1 oz = 28g
Rolled oats 1 cup = 3.25 oz = 90g
Dry milk 1 cup = 3.5 oz = 98g
Granulated sugar 1tsp.= 4g 1c.= 7 oz=196g. 1lb. = 2c.
Brown sugar, packed 1cup = 7 oz=196g 1lb.= 2 1/4 cup
Powdered (6X) sugar, sifted 1c=4 oz=112g. 1lb = 4 1/2 c
Raisins 1 cup = 5 1/4 oz
Fresh or frozen blueberries 1 cup = 5.25 oz = 147g
Chopped nuts 1 cup = 3.75 oz = 105g
Vegetable shortening 1 cup = 6.75 oz
Butter 1 cup = 8 oz = 2 sticks
Baking Soda 1 tsp = 1/16 oz = 4.7g

Baking powder 1 tsp. = 1/8 oz = 3.5g
Salt 1 tsp. = 1/6 oz = 4.7g
Cinnamon, cloves, nutmeg 1 Tbsp. = 1/12 oz = 2.3g
Active dry or instant yeast 1pkg.= 2 1/4 tsp. = 7g

Fluid Ingredients
Honey 1 cup = 12 oz
Maple Syrup 1 cup = 11.5 oz
Vegetable oil 1 cup = 7 oz
Molasses 1 cup = 11 oz
Water or Vinegar 1 cup = 8 oz
Milk 1 cup = 8.5 oz
Whole egg, large* 1 egg = 1 2/3 oz = 10 per lb.
Fluid eggs 1 cup = 5 eggs = 8 oz
Egg white 1 white = 1 oz = 8 oz whites = 1 cup = 8 oz
Egg Yolk 1 yolk = ~2/3oz 12 yolks = 8 oz = 1 cup
*Large eggs are standard size used for home baking

Oven Temperatures

F	C	GAS
225	110	1/4
250	130	1/2
275	140	1
300	150	2
325	170	3
350	180	4
375	190	5
400	200	6
425	220	7

450 230 8
475 240 9

Introduction

I grew up in the south of England at a time when most Mums still stayed at home and looked after the house and kids. My Mum loved to bake - cakes, pies, scones, tarts and puddings.
My happiest memories are of sitting in the kitchen watching the weighing and measuring, mixing and pouring, kneading and rolling. Waiting patiently until it was time to lick the mixing bowl clean.

Baking is almost a lost art form. Store bought cakes are the norm these days. But homemade cakes can't be surpassed for taste, economy and most of all, the pleasure of feeding good food to your family. There are so many additives; preservatives, colorings, chemicals and worst of all, high fructose corn syrup in commercial products. Home baked cakes are just so much healthier and you will know exactly what went into each and every bite.

So give it a go. It's easy, fun, and so rewarding.

I would like to thank Maz for designing my book cover and providing the pictures in this book. http://www.artbymaz.com

Section 1. Cakes

Victoria Sandwich Sponge Cake

The Victoria sandwich, or Victoria sponge as it is also known, was named after Queen Victoria. It consists of two layers of light sponge cake sandwiched together with jam, and sometimes whipped cream or buttercream.

There are two ways to make this delicious cake. The original recipe suggests 4 eggs which you weigh in their shells and then use the same weight in butter, flour and sugar. Or, you can simply use the following proportions.

6 oz caster/fine sugar
6 oz soft butter
1 teaspoon vanilla essence
3 large eggs at room temperature
6 oz self raising flour
1-2 tablespoons of milk
4-5 tablespoons raspberry jam
Optional - ¼ pint/140ml double cream, lightly whipped
icing or confectioners' sugar for dusting

Preheat the oven to 350F.

Grease and line two 8in sandwich pans.

Beat the sugar, butter and vanilla essence until pale and light, then beat in the eggs a little at a time to make a mousse-like consistency. You can do this with an electric mixer.

Fold in the flour by hand (don't beat it in or the cake may be tough). Add enough milk to make a dropping consistency. (Hold a spoon loaded with mixture sideways, and give a sharp jerk of the wrist. Some of the mixture should fall off.)

Divide between the prepared pans, spreading out the mix gently.

Bake for about 25 minutes until well risen and golden brown. Cool in the pan for 10 minutes before turning out on to a rack to cool.

Spread the underside of one cake generously with jam and top with the whipped cream if using. Lay the second sponge on top, topside up. Dust with icing or confectioners' sugar and serve.

Honey and Orange Tea Loaf

6 oz self raising flour
6 oz honey
1 oz butter or margarine
1 egg
1 level teaspoon baking powder
6 tablespoons milk
grated rind of 1 orange
pinch of salt
clear honey to glaze

Set oven 350F.
Grease and line 2lb. loaf pan.

Cream butter and honey together in a bowl, mixing thoroughly. Add the egg and beat vigorously.

Sieve flour, salt and baking powder and add alternately with the milk into creamed mixture.

Sprinkle in the orange rind and mix well.

Spoon into baking pan.

Bake for 45 minutes.

Remove from oven, glaze with honey and return to oven for 10 more minutes.

Remove from pan and cool on wire rack.

Serve sliced and buttered.

Cut and Come Again Cake

This is a delicious, moist fruit cake that was a family favorite for years. If done right, it should have a crumbly, golden brown crust and a rich yellow, fruit-laden interior. It took me years to figure out what the name meant - I thought it was a magic cake that re-grew itself!

1 lb self raising flour
½ level teaspoon salt
1 level teaspoon mixed spice
8 oz granulated sugar
8 oz butter
4 oz currants
4 oz sultanas
optional - few chopped glace cherries
3 medium eggs
just over ¼ pint milk

Heat oven to 375F. Grease and line an 8" - 9" cake pan.

Sieve flour, salt, and mixed spice into a mixing bowl.

Cut butter into small pieces and rub into flour mixture till it resembles breadcrumbs, then stir in sugar and fruit.

Beat eggs and milk together and add to dry ingredients; mix until well blended. (You may need to add a little extra milk if the mixture is too dry.)
Place mixture in pan and bake for 90 minutes, or until firm to the touch and golden brown.

When cool, just cut and come again!

Rock Cakes or Buns

One of the first things we learned to make as kids just because they're so easy to make. Sometimes they resembled "rocks" a little bit more than we intended! The recipe was used a lot during the 2nd World War because it used less eggs than most cake recipes, very important during rationing. One of Harry Potter's favorites!

8 oz self raising flour
4 oz butter
3 oz fine or caster sugar
4 oz dried mixed fruit
1 large egg, lightly beaten
2 to 4 teaspoons milk
A little brown sugar

Preheat oven to 400F. Lightly grease a flat baking sheet.

Sieve flour, salt and mixed spice together. Rub in butter until the mixture resembles fine breadcrumbs, then add the sugar and mixed fruit.

Mix the egg and milk together then pour into the dry mixture. Mix well with a fork to a stiff, rough dough.

Put 12 spoonfuls of the mixture onto the baking sheet and rough up with a fork.

Sprinkle each mound with a little brown sugar.

Bake for 10-15 minutes or until golden brown.

Moist Lemon Cake

8 oz plain flour
4 oz butter
6 oz sugar
2 large eggs
1½ teaspoon baking powder
half teaspoon salt
finely grated rind of 1 lemon
4 oz (120 ml) milk

<u>For the syrup</u>
juice of 1 lemon
3 oz sugar

Preheat oven to 350F. Grease and line an 8 inch round cake pan.

Cream the butter and sugar together until light and fluffy. Add the lemon rind, then beat in the eggs one at a time.

Sift the flour with the baking powder and salt and fold into the mixture with the milk.

Turn the mixture into the prepared pan and bake for 50 minutes to 1 hour until well risen and firm to the touch.

To make the lemon syrup, put the lemon juice and sugar in a small saucepan and heat gently to dissolve.

Turn the cake out on to a wire rack and prick the surface with a fine skewer.

Pour the lemon syrup over the cake and leave until cold.

Note - Make sure you put the syrup on the cake while it's still warm or it will not be absorbed.

Raspberry Buns

8 oz self raising flour
3 oz fine sugar
4 oz butter
1 egg, beaten
¼ cup milk
raspberry jam
fine sugar to dust

Preheat oven to 425F. Grease and flour a baking sheet.

Sift the flour into a bowl and rub in the butter.
Add the sugar and beaten egg with enough milk to make a stiff consistency.

Divide the mixture into about walnut-size balls and place on baking sheet, allowing space for them to spread slightly during cooking.

Make a small hole in the center of each ball and spoon in a little raspberry jam.

Pinch the edges together again. Dust lightly with fine sugar.

Bake for 10 minutes then reduce heat to 350F and bake for a further 5 minutes.

Cool on a wire rack.

Paradise Cake

8 oz shortcrust pastry - homemade or bought
Raspberry jam
4 oz butter
4 oz caster/fine sugar
1 beaten egg
2 tablespoons chopped glacé cherries
2 tablespoons chopped walnuts
2 tablespoons ground almonds
Vanilla essence (extract)
Caster/fine sugar for dusting

Preheat oven to 350F.

Roll out the pastry on a floured surface and use it to line a greased 11 inch by 7 inch baking pan.

Bake this initially on its own.

Cream the butter and sugar together and stir in the beaten egg, cherries, walnuts and almonds.

Add the vanilla essence/extract and mix well.

Spread a layer of raspberry jam on the bottom of the pastry case (after the ten minute baking) and spoon the cake mixture on top of the jam.

Bake for 30/35 minutes.

On removing it from the oven, sprinkle with sugar and leave to cool in the pan.

When cold, remove from the pan and cut into squares.

Marmalade Cake

8 oz self raising flour
2 beaten eggs
3 oz caster sugar
4 oz butter
1 drop vanilla essence/extract)
2 tablespoons orange marmalade
1 teaspoon orange rind, finely grated
2 tablespoons milk
Pinch of salt

Preheat oven to 350F. Grease a 6 inch round cake pan.

Sift the flour and salt into a bowl and rub in the butter until the mixture looks like fine breadcrumbs.

Stir in the sugar, half the orange rind and then add the eggs, marmalade, milk and vanilla. Mix well to achieve the consistency of thick batter.

Pour into pan and bake in the centre of the oven for about one hour and twenty minutes until golden brown and a skewer inserted into the center comes out clean.

Sprinkle the rest of the orange rind on top and allow to rest for a few minutes before you turn out on a wire rack to cool.

Oatmeal Gingerbread

6 oz flour
2 oz oatmeal
2 oz soft brown sugar (light brown sugar)
2 oz butter
2 tablespoons black treacle (molasses)
1 teaspoon of ground ginger
1 teaspoon mixed spice
1 large egg
1 level teaspoon bicarbonate of soda
3 tablespoons milk

Preheat oven to 350F.

Line a seven inch square baking pan with greaseproof paper which has been well buttered.

Melt the butter, sugar and treacle in a saucepan over a gentle heat.

Sieve the flour and bicarbonate of soda into a bowl. Add the oatmeal and spices. Add the melted butter and treacle mixture, a well beaten egg and the milk to the bowl, stirring well until completely blended.

Pour into the baking pan and bake for about 45 minutes.

Allow the cake to cool for ten minutes before turning out onto a wire rack.

Marmalade and Ginger Slice

A delicious mix of the previous 2 cakes.

8 oz flour
8 oz Golden Syrup (see note below)
4 oz butter
8 oz orange marmalade
1 teaspoon baking powder
1 teaspoon ground ginger
1 egg, beaten

Preheat oven to 350F. Grease an 8 inch square cake pan.

Melt the syrup and butter in a pan over a very gentle heat.

Stir in the marmalade and leave to cool.

Sift the dry ingredients into a bowl. Make a well in the center and pour in the syrup mixture and the beaten egg.

Beat well until thoroughly blended.

Turn into the pan and bake for about 45 minutes until firm and golden in color.

Cool on wire rack and cut into slices.

NOTE: Golden Syrup is a British staple. For more information http://en.wikipedia.org/wiki/Golden_syrup. It is available at British stores, some Wholefoods Markets and online.

You can also try an alternative:
Two parts light corn syrup plus one part molasses;
Equal parts honey and corn syrup;
Maple syrup
Dark or light corn syrup

None of these will give you quite the taste and texture that golden syrup does, though.

Traditional British Christmas Cake

No British Christmas is complete without a classic Christmas Cake. The recipe may look complicated but is easy if you prepare and weigh all the ingredients and line the pan before you start. They are usually covered in marzipan and then iced and decorated with Santas, snow men, miniature trees and all kinds of fun things.

A Christmas cake should be made 2 months before Christmas for it to mature and to be fed at regular intervals with brandy. If you are making it later, don't worry, it will still taste good. If you have time, you can also soak the dried mixed fruits the night before in a little extra brandy and proceed with the recipe next day. Creates an even more moist cake.

1lb 2oz currants
8 oz golden raisins or sultanas
8 oz raisins
4 oz mixed candied peel, finely chopped (optional - I hate the stuff!)
6 oz glace cherries, halved
10 oz all-purpose or plain flour
Pinch salt
½ level teaspoon mixed spice
½ level teaspoon ground cinnamon
½ level teaspoon freshly ground nutmeg
10 oz butter, slightly softened
10 oz soft brown sugar
Zest of ½ lemon
6 large eggs, lightly beaten
3 tablespoons brandy, plus extra for feeding

Heat the oven to 300°F.
The temperature is low as the cake needs a long slow bake. It is packed with sugars, fruits and brandy and if the temperature is any higher the outside of the cake will burn and the inside be undercooked.

Line a 9 inch cake pan with 2 thicknesses of parchment or greaseproof paper. Tie a double band of brown or newspaper paper around the outside. This acts as an insulator and to prevent the cake from burning on the outside.
In a large roomy bowl mix the currants, sultanas, raisins, peel and cherries with the flour, salt and spices.

In another large bowl cream the butter with the sugar until light and fluffy. Stir in the lemon zest. Add the beaten egg to the butter mixture a little bit at a time, beating well after each addition - do not try to rush this process as the mixture could curdle. If it does curdle simply add a tbsp of flour and mix again, this should bring the mixture back together. If it doesn't come back together, don't panic, the cake will still be delicious.

Carefully fold in half the flour and fruit into the egg and butter mixture. Once incorporated repeat with the remaining flour and fruit. Finally add the brandy.
Spoon the cake mixture into the prepared cake pan making sure there are no air pockets. Once filled, smooth the surface with the back of a spoon. Make a slight dip in the center - this will rise back up again during cooking and create a smooth surface for icing the cake.

Finally, using a piece of paper towel clean up any smears of cake batter on the greaseproof wrapping. If left on they will burn, and though it won't affect the cake, it doesn't smell too good.

Stand the pan on a double layer of newspaper in the lower part of the oven, if you have a gas oven ensure the paper is well away from the flame, and bake for 4½ hours. If the cake is browning too rapidly, cover the pan with a double layer of greaseproof or parchment paper after 2½ hours. During the cooking time avoid opening the oven door too often as this may cause the cake to collapse.

After 4½ hours check the cake is cooked. The cake should be nicely risen and a deep brown all over. Insert a skewer or fine knife into the centre of the cake. If there is sticky dough on the skewer when you pull it out it needs cooking longer, if it is clean, the cake's done and remove from the oven.

Leave the cake to cool in the pan on a wire rack for an hour, then remove from the pan and leave to cool completely. Once cooled prick the surface of the cake with a fine metal skewer and slowly pour over 2 - 3 tbsp brandy. This feeding should be repeated every two weeks until Christmas. The cake should be stored wrapped in greaseproof or parchment paper in an airtight container. If you would like to ice the cake I recommend searching online for ideas and directions.

Battenberg Cake

No cake is more British than a frivolous Battenberg cake. There is something cheering about the distinctive pink and yellow squares tightly wrapped in a thick layer of marzipan that no other cake seems able to achieve.

Battenberg cake is believed to have been named in honor of the marriage of Queen Victoria's granddaughter to Prince Louis of Battenberg in 1884. Battenberg was my sister's absolute favorite cake when we were kids. I used to pick the marzipan off mine and just eat the cake!

5¼ oz butter, softened, plus extra for greasing
5¼ oz fine/caster sugar
3 large eggs, beaten
1 teaspoon vanilla extract
5¼ oz self raising flour
1 fl oz milk
2 drops of pink food coloring
2¾ oz apricot jam, warmed with 2 drops of water
7 oz marzipan, ready rolled

Preheat the oven to 400F.

In a large bowl beat together the butter and sugar until light and creamy. Slowly add the beaten eggs, beating constantly. Add the vanilla extract and stir.

Sieve the flour into the bowl and continue beating until smooth. Place half of the mixture in another bowl, add the food coloring a little at a time until you have a color you like and stir well.

Grease a 6" square cake pan and divide into 2 by placing a thick layer of aluminum foil down the center. Put the pink mixture into one side and the plain cake into the other.

Place in the oven for 25-30 minutes, or until the cake springs back when pressed lightly. Remove from the oven and leave to cool on a wire rack.

Cut each cake to the same size, then cut each cake in half lengthways. Take a pink cake and brush one side with the warmed jam. Place a yellow piece next to it, jam side together and push gently together.

Brush the top surface with jam and place a piece of yellow cake atop a pink piece and vice versa. Brush all the outside edges with more jam.

Brush the rolled marzipan with a little jam and wrap it all around the cake, hiding the seam underneath. Trim away any excess. Chill in the refrigerator for at least an hour, then serve.

British Fairy Cakes

So easy to make and great to do this with a child. I always loved these. For variation you can make them into Butterfly Cakes by slicing a little off the top of each cake, cut the slivers in half, spread a little buttercream on each cake and place the split top back on like wings.

Makes 12 - 14

4 oz self-raising flour
a pinch of salt
4 oz butter
4 oz sugar
2 eggs

Preheat oven to 350F.

Cream the fat and sugar together until light and fluffy.
Beat the eggs until liquid, then beat into the mixture gradually.

Gently fold in the flour and salt.

Divide the mixture evenly between 12 - 14 paper cases or greased muffin/bun pans, and bake for 15 - 20 minutes.

Note: If using paper cases, place them in dry muffin/bun pans before baking.

Never-Fail Boiled Fruit Cake

There are variations of this recipe and you can pretty much make it with whatever dried fruit you like and any type of sugar and flour. It is moist, keeps well and is so easy to make.

12 oz mixed dried fruit
8 fl oz mixed fruit juice and water, or use brandy or sherry if you prefer
4 oz butter
4 oz brown sugar
1 teaspoon ground mixed spice (U.S. allspice)
4 oz self raising, wholewheat, or white flour
4 oz plain wholemeal or white flour
1 teaspoon bicarbonate of soda
2 eggs, beaten

Put the dried fruit in a saucepan with the liquid, butter, sugar and mixed spice.

Slowly bring to the boil and simmer gently for 2 minutes. Remove from the heat and leave to cool for about 1 hour.

Preheat the oven to 350F. Grease and line an 8 inch round cake pan.

Put the flours and bicarbonate of soda into a mixing bowl. Add the fruit mixture with the eggs and mix thoroughly until evenly blended. It will be quite sloppy.

Pour into the cake pan and bake for 15 minutes, then lower the temperature to 325F.

Bake for a further 1 hour or until a skewer inserted in the center comes out clean.

Turn out onto a wire cooling rack.

Parkin

Parkin is a soft cake traditionally made of oatmeal and molasses, which originated in northern England. Essentially a sticky form of gingerbread, Parkin is traditionally eaten on Bonfire Night, 5 November, but is also enjoyed year-round.

8 oz butter
4 oz soft, dark brown sugar
2 oz black treacle/molasses
7 oz golden syrup/corn syrup
5 oz medium oatmeal
7 oz self raising flour
1 teaspoon baking powder
4 teaspoon ground ginger
2 teaspoon nutmeg
1 teaspoon mixed spice
2 large eggs, beaten
2 tablespoons milk

Preheat oven to 275F. Grease an 8" x 8" square cake pan.

In a large heavy-based saucepan melt together the butter, sugar, treacle and golden syrup over a gentle heat. Do not allow the mixture to boil.

In a large, spacious, mixing bowl stir together all the dry ingredients. Gradually add the melted butter mixture stirring to coat all the dry ingredients and mix thoroughly.

Beat in the eggs a few tablespoons at a time. Finally add the milk and stir well.

Pour the mixture into the prepared tin and cook for 1½ hours until firm and set and a dark golden brown.

Remove the Parkin from the oven and leave to cool in the tin. Once cool store the Parkin in an airtight tin for a minimum of 3 days. If you can resist eating it, you can even leave it up to a week and the flavors really develop and the mixture softens even further and becomes moist and sticky.

The Parkin will keep up to two weeks in an airtight container.

Tantallon Cakes

These little cakes are like a mix of a scone and shortbread - more of a biscuit or cookie than a cake. Originally from Scotland, they are delicious buttered straight from the oven or served with jam and cream.

4 oz flour
4 oz corn or rice flour
4 oz butter
4 oz caster/fine sugar
⅛ teaspoon bicarbonate of soda
1 level teaspoon grated lemon rind
2 eggs, beaten,
icing or confectioners' sugar for dusting

Preheat oven to 375F. Grease a baking sheet, or line with parchment paper.

Cream the butter and sugar together in a bowl and stir in the lemon rind.

Sift the flours and bicarbonate of soda into a separate bowl.

Gradually add the flour mix and the beaten eggs to the creamed butter in small amounts, mixing well with each addition.

Turn out the dough on to a floured surface, knead gently and roll out to ½ inch thick.

Cut into rounds with a 2½ inch pastry or cookie cutter.

Transfer to baking sheet and bake for 20-25 minutes until light gold.

Cool on a wire rack and dust with icing sugar.

Madeira Cake

This is one of my all time favorite cakes. It's similar to pound cake, but I think it's much tastier. Named for the Madeira wine the cake was traditionally served with, not the very beautiful island of Madeira as some people think! The recipe dates back to the 18th century.

6 oz softened unsalted butter
6 oz caster/fine sugar, plus extra for sprinkling
Grated rind and juice of 1 lemon
6 oz self raising flour
3 oz plain flour, sifted
3 large eggs at room temperature

Preheat the oven to 325F. Grease and line an 8 inch round cake pan or loaf pan.

Cream the butter and sugar, and add the lemon zest.

Add the eggs one at a time with a tablespoon of the flour for each.

Gently fold in the rest of the flour and, finally, the lemon juice.

Sprinkle with caster/fine sugar and bake for 1 hour or until a cake-tester comes out clean.

Place on cooling rack and let cool in the tin before turning out.

Tea Fruit Cake

I remember this was one of the first cakes I made when I first left home and began playing house. So easy, and even though I can't stand tea, I really love this moist, fruity cake.

14 oz dried mixed fruit
10 oz white or brown sugar
10 oz plain flour
1 teaspoon nutmeg
1 teaspoon cinnamon
1 teaspoon baking powder
1 egg, beaten

Make a mug of tea using 2 bags to make it good and strong.

Place the dried fruit in a bowl and pour over the brewed tea.

Let it soak for 2 hours or more, even overnight if you like.

Preheat the oven to 325F.

Mix all the ingredients together in a large mixing bowl, then place into a lightly greased round cake pan and bake for 2 hours.

Place on a wire rack to cool.

Can be served sliced and buttered with, yep, you guessed it, a cup of tea!

Or coffee for me.

Seed Cake

I know, it sounds like a treat for the birds, but this very historical recipe gets a mention in The Hobbit, where it was made by Bilbo and served with a mug of beer.

Made with caraway seeds, a seed cake is a traditional British Isles concoction. Some date it back to English recipes, while others say residents of Ireland or Wales invented it first. Geoffrey Chaucer's Canterbury Tales mentions the seed cake as round and resembling a shield.

6 oz butter
6 oz caster/fine sugar
3 eggs
½ teasoon vanilla extract
1 tablespoon of caraway seeds
1 level tablespoon ground almonds
½ teaspoon baking powder
8 oz plain flour
A little milk

Preheat oven to 350F. Prepare a loaf pan or 8 inch springform pan.

In a large bowl, cream the butter and then add the sugar. When mix is light and fluffy stir in the caraway seeds.

Sift the flour into another bowl and stir in the ground almonds.

Whisk the eggs and vanilla extract together and gradually add to the creamed butter and sugar. Beat well to mix.

Fold in the flour, adding the baking powder mixed in with the last addition of the flour.

Add a little milk or water if needed to make a dropping consistency.

Pour into prepared cake pan.

Bake for 50-60 minutes, remove from oven and let cool in the pan.

Eccles Cakes

An Eccles cake is a small, round cake made from flaky pastry filled with currants and topped with sugar. They are named for the town of Eccles in Lancashire and have been popular since 1793.

Flaky pastry - home made or purchased
1 oz butter
4 oz soft brown sugar
4 oz currants
2 oz chopped candied peel
1 teaspoon ground nutmeg
1 teaspoon mixed spice
milk and fine sugar to glaze

Preheat oven to 425F. Grease a baking sheet. Line with paper too if preferred.

Melt butter in pan and stir in currants, peel sugar and spices. Mix well.

Roll out the pastry to just under ¼ inch thick. Cut into rounds with a 3 inch cookie or pastry cutter.

Place a heaped teaspoon of fruit mixture onto the center of each round.

Moisten the edges of the pastry with water and with your fingertips, draw up the edges of each round so that they meet in the center completely enclosing the filling. Press well together to seal.

Turn each cake over and roll to about ½ inch thick.

Make 3 slits in the top of each with a sharp knife.

Brush with milk and sprinkle thickly with sugar.

Place on baking sheet and bake just above the center for 20 minutes.

Cool on wire rack.

Section 2. Puddings

Puddings are a British institution. The word "pudding" is used to mean dessert, or it can be one dish, sweet or savory, such as Steamed Sponge Pudding, Rice Pudding, or Steak and Kidney Pudding. The word (to us Brits) conjures up images of home. Comfort food; happy memories of family dinners around the table. No good meal was complete without pudding. I wish I had a dollar for every time I've heard the phrase, "What's for pudding?"

I'm sticking to my good old childhood favorite puddings here and since I don't eat meat I won't be including my always detested Steak and Kidney!

Very Proper English Custard

A thick, rich, sweet mixture made by gently cooking together egg yolks, sugar, milk or cream, and sometimes other flavorings. Custard can be served as a hot sauce, poured over dessert, or as a cold layer in, for example, a trifle. When it is cold, it 'sets' and becomes firm. You can't have a traditional English pud without a good dollop of delicious custard poured all over it. Most Brits make custard the easy way using a ready made powder called Bird's Custard which is just mixed with milk and sugar. It tastes great but not as great as home made from scratch. It's not difficult so give it a go!

1 pint milk
2fl oz single cream
½ teaspoon vanilla extract
4 egg yolks
1 oz caster/fine sugar
2 level teaspoons cornflour

Bring the milk, cream and vanilla pod to simmering point slowly over a low heat.

Whisk the yolks, sugar and cornflour together in a bowl until well blended.
Pour the hot milk and cream on to the eggs and sugar, whisking all the time with a balloon whisk.

Return to the pan, add vanilla extract and over a low heat gently stir with a wooden spatula until thickened.

Pour the custard into a jug and serve at once.

To keep hot, stand the jug in a pan of hot water and cover the top with cling film to prevent a skin forming.

To use cold, pour into a bowl and stand it over a bowl of ice. Stir frequently until cold to prevent a skin forming.

Spotted Dick

A very traditional English winter pudding the name of which is sure to raise a smile or two. The earliest recipes for spotted dick are from 1847. For non-British readers, "spotted dick" is a boiled suet pudding, with bits of dried fruit (usually raisins or currants) that look like little spots. I always preferred the other name of Spotted Dog Pudding, just because I've always loved dogs, especially spotty ones! In order to get the texture right it has to be made with suet. If you can't find any locally it can be bought online. It freezes well too.

4 oz raisins
2 oz currants,
3 oz dark brown sugar
Grated zest of 1 unwaxed lemon
8 oz self-raising flour plus extra for dusting
4 oz shredded <u>suet</u>
Pinch of salt
2 fl oz milk

In a small bowl mix the raisins, currants, sugar and lemon rind for the filling.

Sift the flour into a large mixing bowl; add the suet and the salt and rub together to combine. Add a little milk and using a knife cut through the mixture, adding more milk little by little until it comes together. Finally use your hands to combine into a soft, elastic dough. Add more milk if necessary.

Place the dough on a lightly floured surface and roll into a rectangle about 8 x 12 inches. Evenly spread the pudding filling mixture over the dough leaving a ½ inch border. Paint the border with a little cold water. Roll up carefully from the narrow end. Soak a clean tea towel or cloth napkin in boiling water for a few minutes, squeeze to remove excess water. Wrap the suet roll pudding in the napkin twisting at each end and securing with kitchen string. Steam for 2 hours in a steamer. Alternatively, wrap the pudding suet roll in foil and bake in a hot oven, 400F for 1 hour 30 mins.

Unwrap immediately, cut into thick slices and serve in warmed bowls with lashings of custard.

Bakewell Pudding

Sometimes called Bakewell Tart this recipe apparently began as a mistake when the cook at the Rutland Arms in Bakewell, Derbyshire, put the egg and almond mixture on top of the jam instead of the pastry. I love happy accidents!

3 large eggs
8oz caster sugar
8oz butter
4oz ground almonds
Puff pastry
Raspberry Jam
Optional - flaked almonds for top

Preheat the oven to 425F.

Line two deep 8" pans with puff pastry and spread the bottoms with raspberry jam.

Beat the eggs till pale and runny, but not too frothy.

Melt the butter and let it cool a bit, then add it to the egg mixture. Stir in the almonds and sugar. Then pour into the pastry cases. If desired, top with sliced almonds.

Bake for 10 minutes, then reduce the heat to 350F and bake for a further 20 minutes.

Let them cool down, eat one, freeze the other. They freeze very well.

Delicious with custard!

Treacle Tart

Sweet, sticky and delicious! One of the most well known and popular of all traditional English puddings. You do need Golden Syrup to make this taste authentic, but if you can't find any then you could use corn syrup. If you don't want to make pastry use ready made or a pie crust.

8 oz shortcrust pastry
8 oz golden syrup
8 oz white breadcrumbs
1 heaped tablespoon black treacle or molasses (blackstrap if preferred)
2 or 3 tablespoons lemon juice

Preheat oven to 350F.

Roll out the pasty and line an 8 inch flan or pie dish.

Sprinkle the breadcrumbs evenly over the pastry base.

Warm the syrup and treacle very gently in a saucepan over a low heat. Stir in the lemon juice. Pour over the breadcrumbs.

Cook for 25 to 30 minutes until golden brown.

Serve hot or cold with whipped cream, vanilla ice cream or creme fraiche. We also love it with custard.

Apple Crumble

So easy to make and perfect with custard or ice cream. You can use different fruit with this recipe or add extra ingredients such as sultanas, raisins, blackberries etc.

4 lbs granny smith or sharp green apples, peeled, cored and sliced
1 cup sugar
2 cups all-purpose flour
4 oz butter
1 teaspoon cinnamon or allspice
1 pinch salt

Preheat oven to 400°F.

Place sliced apples in a greased 13" X 9" dish.

Sprinkle ½ cup of sugar and ½ teaspoon of the cinnamon over fruit.

In a medium bowl, stir together flour, remaining ½ teaspoon cinnamon and salt. Rub butter into flour until mixture resembles breadcrumbs.

Stir in remaining ½ cup of sugar. Sprinkle over fruit.

Bake at 400F for 30-45 minutes, or until top is lightly browned.

Jam Roly-Poly

This is a very traditional English pudding and, along with most Brits, one of my childhood favorites. It is a flat-rolled suet pudding, which is then spread with jam and rolled up. Dating from about 1847, Jam Roly-Poly was also known as shirt-sleeve pudding because it was often steamed and served in an old shirt-sleeve. Because of this, another nickname for the pudding was dead-man's arm. Lovely!

8 oz self raising flour
pinch of salt
4 oz shredded suet
6-8 tablespoons water
4 tablespoons raspberry jam, warmed
a little milk
1 egg, beaten
fine sugar to glaze

Preheat oven to 400F. Grease a baking sheet.

Sift the flour into a bowl with the salt. Add the suet and sufficient water to create a soft but not sticky dough. Turn on to a floured board and roll out to a rectangle about 8x12 inch.

Brush the pastry with the warmed jam, leaving a ½ inch border all round. Fold in this border and brush with milk. With the short side towards you, roll up the pastry loosely and seal the ends well.

Place on greased baking sheet, with the sealed edge underneath. Brush with the beaten egg and sprinkle with caster sugar.

Bake for 35-40 minutes until golden brown.

Remove from the oven, sprinkle on a little more sugar and serve hot with custard.

Manchester Tart

The Manchester tart is a traditional English baked tart, which consists of a shortcrust pastry shell spread with raspberry jam, covered with a custard filling and topped with flakes of coconut.

1 pint milk
4 oz shortcrust pastry, or a ready made sweet pastry case
flour for dusting
3 or 4 tablespoons strawberry, blackcurrant, apricot or raspberry jam
3 or 4 tablespoons custard powder
½ cup desiccated coconut
1 tablespoon sugar

Preheat oven to 400F.

On a clean dry surface dusted with flour, roll out the pastry to about ⅛ inch.

Grease a round 9 inch baking pan and place pastry into it, gently pressing into edges. Prick base with a fork and put baking parchment or greaseproof paper on top of the pastry and weigh down with dried beans.

Bake "blind" or without filling, for 20 minutes.

Remove from oven and allow to cool.

Spread jam over the pastry base. Sprinkle half the coconut over the jam.

Boil the milk and pour into a bowl with the sugar and custard powder.
Beat well until it has a thick creamy consistency.

Pour onto the pastry.

Sprinkle with coconut and sugar and allow to cool.

Slice and serve.

For variation add a layer of thinly sliced banana over the jam.

British Sticky Toffee Pudding

A decadent baked date pudding topped with a soft caramel toffee sauce. Should come with a warning sign! So addictive……...mmmm.

Pudding
2 cups boiling water
8 oz (just short of 2 cups after chopping) dates, fresh or dried, pitted and chopped
1 teaspoon bicarbonate of soda
8 oz flour
6 oz caster/fine sugar
2 oz butter
1 teaspoon baking powder
1 medium egg
1 teaspoon vanilla essence

Sauce
2 oz butter
3 oz soft brown sugar
3 or 4 tablespoons double or single cream

First pour the boiling water over the dates and bicarbonate of soda and leave to stand.

Preheat the oven to 350F.

Cream the butter and sugar together in a bowl until pale in color. Gradually stir in the egg, flour and baking powder.

Stir in the dates with the liquid and add the vanilla essence.

Pour into a greased 2½ pint ovenproof dish and bake for about 40 minutes until risen and firm to the touch.

Make the sauce by boiling the ingredients together for 2 minutes and pour over the warm pudding.

Serve with whipped cream or vanilla ice cream. YUM!

Chocolate Fudge Pudding

A chocolate sponge pudding with a deliciously sticky chocolate sauce.

Pudding
4 oz butter
4 oz caster/fine sugar
2 medium eggs
3 oz self-raising flour
3 tablespoons cocoa powder
½ teaspoon vanilla essence
2 tablespoons milk

Sauce
4 oz soft brown sugar
3 tablespoons cocoa powder
½ pint boiling water

Preheat oven to 375F.

Place all the pudding ingredients into a bowl and beat well to a soft consistency, or use a mixer or food processor.

Pour into a 2½ pint ovenproof dish.

Make the sauce by combining the sugar and cocoa in a bowl and adding the hot water. Mix well.

Pour the sauce over the pudding mixture.

Bake for 40 minutes.

Turn out the pudding onto a plate and a thick chocolate sauce will have formed coating the light sponge pudding.

Serve with thick fresh cream.

Traditional English Sherry Trifle

Trifle recipes date back to the 16th century. This pudding is made from thick (or often solidified) custard, fruit, sponge cake, sherry or fruit juice, and whipped cream. These ingredients are usually arranged in alternating layers. It's a great way to use up stale cake or use store bought butter or madeira cake.

If you don't want to use sherry you can substitute fruit juice.

8 -12 oz stale sponge or one store bought butter pound or madeira cake (depends on how much cake you like - I like lots)
4 tablespoons raspberry jam
6 tablespoons sweet sherry
raspberries - one can, or 12 oz frozen partially thawed or 12 oz fresh
¾ pint whipping cream
2 oz flaked almonds, toasted
1 pint custard allowed to cool

Split the sponge in half lengthways then spread each half thinly with raspberry jam. Sandwich each half back together and cut into quarters.

Place in the base of a 3½ pint glass bowl.

Sprinkle the sherry over the sponge and spoon over the raspberries and their juice.
Chill for 3-4 hours or overnight.

Spoon the cold custard onto the raspberries spreading to the edges with a palette knife.

Gently whip the cream until it nearly holds its shape, then spoon three quarters of it on top of the custard and carefully spread to the sides of the bowl.

Whip the remaining cream until it holds it shape.

Pipe swirls of cream around the top of the bowl and decorate with flaked almonds.

Bread Pudding

An old fashioned pudding to use up stale bread. The thrifty British have so many recipes for leftovers! I remember my Dad loved to make huge batches of this. I can still picture him mixing this up in the dishwashing bowl because there was nothing else big enough. The mixture would come up to his elbows. We all used to eat it despite the unique preparation!

8 oz stale bread, white or wholemeal
½ pint milk
4 oz currants or sultanas
3 oz brown sugar
½ teaspoon ground mixed spice (U.S. allspice)
4 oz melted butter
1 egg
caster/fine sugar for topping

Preheat oven to 350F. Grease a 2 to 2½ pint ovenproof dish

Cut away any hard crusts from the bread, break into pieces and put into the milk to soak for 30 to 60 minutes.

Squeeze out the excess milk from the bread, put it into a bowl and break up any lumps with a wooden spoon.

Add in all the other ingredients and mix well, adding a little milk if necessary, to produce a soft, dropping consistency.

Put into the baking dish, spread out and bake for about 1 hour until golden brown.

Remove from the oven and sprinkle with caster sugar.

Serve hot with custard or cold, sliced.

Glastonbury Pudding

This recipe originates in Somerset, where the cider apples grow. A delicious sponge pudding layered with apricots, apples and apricot jam.

Sponge
4 oz butter
4 oz caster/fine sugar
2 medium eggs
6 oz wholemeal self-raising flour
grated rind of half a lemon

Filling
1 medium cooking apple, peeled, cored and coarsely grated
3 oz no soak dried apricots, finely chopped
4 tablespoons apricot jam
juice of half a lemon

Grease a 1½ pint pudding basin.

Prepare the sponge mixture either by the traditional creaming method and flavoring with the lemon rind, or by putting all the ingredients into a food processor and mixing for about 30 seconds.

Mix together all the filling ingredients.

Place a layer of sponge mixture into the base of the pudding basin and top with some of the filling. Continue alternating the layers and finish with a layer of sponge mixture.

Cover with a circle of greaseproof paper and then cover and seal with kitchen foil.

Steam for 2 hours.

Remove covering and leave the pudding in the basin for 5 minutes before turning out onto a warm serving dish. Serve hot with custard or cream.

Bread and Butter Pudding

Bread and Butter Pudding (not to be confused with Bread Pudding) is one of England's most loved and traditional desserts. When made in the traditional way, it's rich, warming and filling and perfect for cold winter nights. So easy, and can be made with any stale bread, brioche, or even croissants.

8 to 10 slices well-buttered bread
2 oz sultanas
2 oz raisins
4 eggs
1 oz sugar
20 fl.oz. Milk
1 teaspoon vanilla
A little extra sugar

Preheat the oven to 325F. Grease a deep ovenproof dish.

Remove the crusts from the buttered bread (I usually like to leave the crusts on because they get nice and chewy) and cut into quarters, triangles or squares.

Reserve 4 quarters for the top and arrange the rest in layers in the dish, sprinkling the sultanas and raisins between each layer. Top with the reserved quarters.

In a saucepan, heat the milk to hot but not boiling. In a large bowl, mix together the eggs and sugar then add the hot milk and vanilla, stirring well.

Slowly strain over the bread and fruit, being careful not to dislodge the top layer of bread. Leave the bread and butter pudding to stand for 10 minutes.

Sprinkle with a little sugar and bake in the oven for 30-40 minutes until the top is browned and crispy.

Figgy Pudding

An old English Victorian tradition usually served after Christmas dinner. It's a rich and fruity sponge pudding flavored with brandy, rum or fortified wine. In our house Dad always put some (washed) coins in and we would have to be careful how we ate it in case we swallowed one. Usually there would be threepenny bits and sixpences and maybe one big half-crown. Funny, Mum always got the half-crown…..I think Dad cheated somehow!

8 oz dried figs
2 oz raisins
3 oz butter
3 oz soft brown sugar
3 oz flour
2 oz fresh white breadcrumbs
1 oz ground almonds
pinch mixed spice
grated rind of ½ a lemon
1 egg
3 or 4 tablespoons brandy, rum, madeira or sherry

Soak the figs and raisins overnight in cold weak tea, to which a little lemon juice has been added. Next morning, drain the fruit well and chop the figs finely.

Cream the butter and sugar together in a bowl and then fold in the flour a little at a time. Add the breadcrumbs, ground almonds, spice, lemon rind, figs and raisins and combine well.

Beat the egg with whichever alcohol you prefer and add to the mixture, stirring well. Pour into a 1½ to 2 pint buttered pudding basin, cover with buttered greaseproof paper and seal with kitchen foil.

Steam for 3½ to 4 hours, topping up the water as necessary until the pudding is springy and well risen.

Turn out onto a warm plate.
Serve with custard or thick fresh cream.

Marmalade Pudding

A marmalade sponge pudding served with a tangy marmalade sauce.

Pudding
4 tablespoons orange marmalade
4 oz self-raising flour
4 oz caster/fine sugar
4 oz butter
1 level teaspoon baking powder
2 medium eggs
grated rind of 1 orange

Sauce
5 tablespoons orange marmalade
¼ pint water/orange juice mix
2 level teaspoons arrowroot
2 to 3 tablespoons cold water

Grease a 2 pint pudding basin and place 4 tablespoons of marmalade on the base.

Put the flour, sugar, butter, baking powder, eggs and orange rind into a large bowl.
Mix and beat well for 2 - 3 minutes until soft and smooth.

Put on top of the marmalade in the basin.

Cover with a circle of greaseproof paper and then seal with kitchen foil.

Steam for 2 hours.

Prepare the sauce by warming together in a pan the marmalade and water/orange juice and simmer for 5 minutes.

Blend the arrowroot and cold water to a smooth cream and stir in some of the marmalade mix.

Return to the pan and heat, stirring until the sauce thickens and clears.

Turn out the pudding onto a warm plate and serve hot with the sauce.

Belvoir House Pudding

A delicious steamed sponge pudding flavored with sherry. Originates from the Leicestershire home of the Dukes of Rutland. By the way, Belvoir is pronounced "beaver" - no really, don't laugh!

4 oz butter
4 oz caster sugar
2 eggs, beaten
4 oz flour
1/2 teaspoon baking powder
1 pinch salt
2 oz glace cherries, chopped
½ oz angelica, chopped
2 tablespoons coffee essence
OR
3 tablespoons cold black coffee and 3 tablespoons rum or sherry

Preheat oven to 350F. Grease a 1½ to 2 pint ovenproof dish.

In a bowl, cream the butter until soft, then add the sugar, mixing until light and fluffy. Beat in the eggs, a little at a time.

Sift the flour, baking powder and salt together, and fold into the mixture. Mix the cherries and angelica together and stir in, with the coffee essence or black coffee and the rum or sherry.

Turn into the dish or a fluted cake pan and bake for 35-40 minutes until well risen and springy, covering the top with a piece of kitchen foil if it appears to be browning too quickly.

Turn out on to a warm serving dish and serve with rum or sherry flavored whipped cream or custard.

Ginger and Pear Upside-down Pudding

Popular in Victorian times this ginger sponge pudding comes out topped with pears and walnuts coated with butterscotch. Delicious!

6 oz flour
1 teaspoon bicarbonate of soda
½ teaspoon salt
1 teaspoon ground ginger
1 teaspoon ground cinnamon
3 oz butter
4 oz soft brown sugar
4 oz treacle or molasses
¼ pint milk
1 medium egg, beaten

Topping
2 oz butter 4 oz soft brown sugar
8 to 12 walnut halves
1 medium can pears in natural sauce, about 4 pears

Preheat oven to 350F. Grease an 8 inch, deep cake pan.

Prepare the topping: cream together the butter and sugar and spread evenly over the base of the pan. Arrange the pear halves on top, cut side down and place the walnuts prettily around them.

Put the flour, bicarbonate of soda, salt, ginger, and cinnamon into a large bowl.

Heat together in a pan the butter, sugar and treacle/molasses until the butter has melted, but do not boil. Stir in the milk and egg.

Beat the liquid ingredients into the flour until smooth and pour onto the pears and walnuts.

Bake for about 1 hour. Turn out and serve warm with whipped double cream.

Traditional Rice Pudding

Nothing quite like this good old British staple after a good old sunday roast. My sister and I used to take a little run around the garden after dinner so we would have room for the rice pud!

4 oz short grain pudding rice
¾ pint single cream
¾ pint full cream milk
2 oz caster/fine sugar
freshly grated nutmeg
1 vanilla pod (optional)
1 oz unsalted butter

Preheat the oven to 300F. Grease a 2½ pint ovenproof dish with a little butter.

Rinse the rice under cold water and place in the ovenproof dish.

Place the cream, milk, sugar and a generous grating of nutmeg in a medium saucepan. Scrape in the seeds of the vanilla pod, if using. Heat gently until almost simmering, then remove from the heat and pour over the rice, stirring well.

Dot the butter over the top and place in the oven for 1½ hours, stirring after the first 30 minutes (at this stage, you can add an extra grating of nutmeg, if liked).

If the pudding still seems very runny, return to the oven, checking every 10 minutes, until it is loosely creamy but not runny. The cooking time will vary, depending on the type and depth of dish you use.

When the pudding is golden brown on top and has a soft, creamy texture, remove from the oven and allow to rest for 10 minutes before serving.

Can also be eaten with a spoonful of jam, which is how it was always served for school dinners. Delicious!

Chester Pudding

A sweet pastry tart filled with almond paste and topped with meringue.

6 oz shortcrust pastry
4 tablespoons butter
1 tablespoon ground almonds
4 tablespoons caster/fine sugar
3 eggs, separated
milk for glazing
1 additional tablespoon caster/fine sugar

Preheat the oven to 375F.

Roll the pastry out on a lightly floured surface and use it to line a pie plate. Decorate the edges of the pastry and brush with a little milk.

Melt the sugar and the butter together in a saucepan and add the almonds. Stir in the yolks of the 3 eggs and one of the egg whites. Heat carefully over a low heat stirring constantly, until the mixture thickens.

Pour into the prepared pastry-lined pie plate and bake for 20 minutes.

Meanwhile, whisk the remaining two egg whites until stiff and then fold in 1 tablespoon of sugar.

After the cooking time, remove the pudding from the oven and cover the top with the egg whites. Return the pudding to the oven on the bottom shelf until the meringue top is set and golden.

Steamed Syrup Sponge Pudding

6oz warm butter
3 tablespoons Golden Syrup
1 tablespoon treacle or molasses
6oz soft brown sugar
zest of 1 lemon
3 large eggs, lightly beaten
6oz self raising flour
1 rounded teaspoon baking powder

Plus you will need foil, baking parchment and string

<u>To serve</u>
3 tablespoons Golden Syrup
custard

Generously butter the inside of a 2 pint pudding basin. Cut a circle about two times larger than the pudding basin diameter, of both baking parchment and aluminum foil

Spoon 3 tablespoons golden syrup into the base of the pudding basin and set aside.

Sift the flour and baking powder into a large mixing bowl. Add the softened butter, eggs, sugar, lemon zest and black treacle. Using an electric hand whisk (or a large fork), beat the mixture for about 2 minutes until it's thoroughly blended.(Add a splash of milk if the mixture is very thick.)

Spoon the mixture into the pudding basin and smooth the surface.

Pleat the baking parchment by folding over an inch of parchment in the centre. Repeat with the foil. This allows for expansion of the pudding as it cooks.

Cover the basin with the circle of baking parchment, with the pleat in the centre of the pudding. Cover the parchment with the circle of aluminum foil, again with the pleat in the centre. Tie the pudding very tightly around the rim with string. Create a carrying handle by tying the excess string across the top of the basin and tying it under the string on the opposite side – this will help you lift the pudding out of the pan once it's cooked. Trim any excess baking paper and aluminum foil, leaving a 1in border, and turn the edges in on themselves to seal.

Put an upturned heatproof saucer or small trivet in a large, deep saucepan, and place the pudding basin on top. Add enough just-boiled water to the pan to come halfway up the sides of the basin. Cover the pan with a tight-fitting lid and place over a low heat. Allow to steam in the gently simmering water for 1¾ hours, adding more water to the pan if necessary. (Make sure the pan does not boil dry.)

If you would prefer, you can cook the pudding in a crockpot/slow cooker. It will take about 3 to 4 hours.

The pudding is done when a skewer inserted into the centre of the pudding (through the aluminum foil and baking paper) comes out clean. When done, turn off the heat and carefully lift the basin from the water. Leave to stand for 5 minutes.

Cut the string from the basin and discard the aluminum foil and paper. Run a cutlery knife around the edge of the pudding to loosen the sides, carefully invert onto a deep plate and remove the basin.

Spoon the extra syrup over the pudding, cut into wedges and serve with custard.

Monmouth Pudding

7 fl oz milk
7 oz white breadcrumbs.
¾ oz softened unsalted butter
grated zest of 1 lemon
4 oz raspberries
3 oz caster/fine sugar
2 eggs, separated
1 egg white
sifted icing/confectioners' sugar to dust

Raspberry sauce
4 oz raspberries
1 tablespoon icing/confectioners' sugar, sifted

Preheat the oven to 275F. Lightly butter a 2 pint baking dish.

Heat the milk until scalding hot, but not quite boiling. Put the breadcrumbs into a large, heatproof bowl and pour over the hot milk.

Stir in the butter and lemon zest, then leave to cool for 10-15 minutes or until the crumbs have absorbed the milk. Meanwhile, put the raspberries in a mixing bowl. Sprinkle over 1 oz of the caster/fine sugar and mash with a fork to make a thick, rough mixture. Spread over the bottom of the baking dish.

Stir the egg yolks into the cooled breadcrumb mixture.

Put the 3 egg whites into a clean bowl and whisk until stiff peaks form, then whisk in the remaining 2 oz caster/fine sugar.

With a large metal spoon, gently fold the egg whites into the breadcrumb mixture and spoon on top of the raspberries.
Bake for 40-45 minutes or until the pudding is set and lightly golden.

Meanwhile, make the sauce.

Purée the raspberries by pressing them through a nylon sieve. Stir in the icing/confectioners' sugar, then pour into a serving jug. Remove the pudding from the oven and leave to cool slightly, then dust the top with icing/confectioners' sugar.

Serve warm, with the raspberry sauce and fresh cream, creme fraiche or vanilla ice cream.

Chocolate Bread and Butter Pudding

This is the MOST divine, delicious and decadent dessert, and ridiculously easy to make.

9 slices ¼ inch thick white bread, preferably one day old
5 oz 70% dark chocolate in small pieces
3 oz butter
15 fl oz whipping cream
4 oz caster/fine sugar
3 large eggs
4 tablespoons dark rum
pinch of cinnamon

Remove the crusts from the bread so you have 9 pieces about 4 inches square. Cut each slice into 4 triangles.

Place the chocolate, whipping cream, rum, sugar, butter and cinnamon in a bowl set over a saucepan of barely simmering water, being careful not to let the bowl touch the water.

Wait until the butter and chocolate have melted and the sugar has completely dissolved, remove the bowl from the heat and give it a really good stir to amalgamate all the ingredients.

In a separate bowl, whisk the eggs. Pour the chocolate mixture over them and whisk again very thoroughly to blend them together.

Spoon about a ½ inch layer of the chocolate mixture into the base of the dish and arrange half the bread triangles over the chocolate in overlapping rows.

Pour half the remaining chocolate mixture all over the bread as evenly as possible, then arrange the rest of the triangles over that, finishing off with a layer of chocolate. Use a fork to press the bread gently down so that it gets evenly covered with the liquid as it cools.

Cover the dish with Saranwrap or clingfilm and allow to stand at room temperature for 2 hours before transferring it to the fridge for a minimum of 24 (but preferably 48) hours before cooking.

When you're ready to cook the pudding, preheat the oven to 350F. Remove the Saranwrap and bake in the oven on a high shelf for 30-35 minutes, by which time the top will be crunchy and the inside soft and gooey.

Leave it to stand for 10 minutes before serving with cold double cream poured over.

Section 3. Scones

The Great British Scone; once tasted, never forgotten. Plain, unadorned and simple, scones are a quintessential part of the British way of life. Scones should be enjoyed straight from the oven, with just a brief pause to add jam and clotted cream. Divine. If the only scone you have ever tasted was bought in a cafe or bakery, then you are in for a treat when you taste the real thing. Home baked perfection.

Sweet or savory scones can be made quickly and easily and they are delicious both hot or cold. If you want to ensure yours are light, fluffy and well risen, just follow these simple rules.

When preparing the equipment and ingredients for making the scones, ensure they are all as cool as possible, including your hands. Butter should be very cold, but not frozen. Warm hands, ingredients, and equipment will melt the butter rather than it being rubbed in, resulting in heavy scones.

Work quickly, and lightly. Avoid over rubbing or kneading the scone mixture. The mixture does not need to be super-smooth, it needs simply to be pulled together in a light, pliable dough.

When cutting the scones using a cookie cutter, avoid twisting the cutter, then gently shake the scone onto the prepared tray. When cutting with a knife, be sure it's sharp. Blunt knives or twisting the cookie cutter tears at the edges of the scone and stunts the rise of the scone.

Cook near the top of the oven, even when using a fan. Scones like it best near the top.

Freshly baked scones should be pulled gently apart with the fingers. Cutting spoils the texture and makes them doughy. As scones stale quickly they are best made and eaten on the same day.

Basic Plain Scones

8 oz self raising flour
2 oz cold butter
1 level teaspoon baking powder
½ tsp salt
¼ pint milk
1 egg beaten with a little milk

Heat the oven to 450F.
Grease and flour a baking sheet, or line with parchment paper.

Sift the flour into a roomy baking bowl then add the butter, baking powder and salt.

Quickly rub the butter into the flour until the mixture resembles fine breadcrumbs.

Make a well in the center and using a dinner knife, stir in enough milk to make a soft, pliable dough.

Turn the mixture onto a floured board and knead very lightly, only 3 or 4 times, until just smooth, then lightly roll out to ¾" thick.

Cut rounds with a 3" cutter or cut into triangles with a sharp knife.

Place on the baking tray and brush with the beaten egg and milk mixture.

Bake near the top of the hot oven for 7 to 10 minutes or until golden brown and well risen.

Cool on a wire rack before eating.

Basic Tea Scones

8 oz self raising flour
1 level teaspoon baking powder
½ level teaspoon salt
2 oz butter
1 oz caster/fine sugar
¼ pint milk
Extra milk for brushing, or egg and milk mixture

Heat the oven to 450F. Grease and flour a baking sheet, or line with parchment paper.

Sift the flour into a roomy baking bowl then add the butter, baking powder and salt.

Quickly rub the butter into the flour until the mixture resembles fine breadcrumbs.

Add sugar and stir.

Make a well in the center and using a dinner knife, stir in enough milk to make a soft, pliable dough.

Turn the mixture onto a floured board and knead very lightly, only 3 or 4 times, until just smooth, then lightly roll out to ¾" thick.

Cut into rounds with a 3" fluted cutter.

Place on the baking tray and brush with milk or beaten egg and milk mixture.

Bake near the top of the hot oven for 7 to 10 minutes or until golden brown and well risen.

Cool on a wire rack before eating.

Serve with butter, or lashings of jam and whipped or clotted cream.

Buttermilk Scones

8 oz self raising flour
½ teaspoon salt
1½ oz butter
¼ pint buttermilk, plus extra for brushing

Heat the oven to 450F.
Grease and flour a baking sheet, or line with parchment paper.

Sift flour and salt into a bowl. Rub butter into flour until mixture resembles fine breadcrumbs. Add buttermilk all at once. Mix to a soft, but not sticky, dough with a knife.

Turn onto a lightly floured surface. Knead quickly until smooth. Roll out to about ½ inch thick. Cut into 7 or 8 rounds with 2½ or 3 inch cookie cutter.

Transfer to baking sheet. Brush tops with milk. Bake for 7-10 minutes or until well risen and golden.

Cool on a wire cooling rack. Serve with butter.

Currant Scones

8 oz self raising flour
1 level teaspoon baking powder
½ level teaspoon salt
2 oz butter
1 oz caster/fine sugar
2 oz currants or raisins
¼ pint milk
Extra milk for brushing, or egg and milk mixture

Heat the oven to 450F.
Grease and flour a baking sheet, or line with parchment paper.

Sift the flour into a roomy baking bowl then add the butter, baking powder and salt.

Quickly rub the butter into the flour until the mixture resembles fine breadcrumbs.

Stir in sugar and currants.

Make a well in the center and using a dinner knife, stir in enough milk to make a soft, pliable dough.

Turn the mixture onto a floured board and knead very lightly, only 3 or 4 times, until just smooth, then lightly roll out to ¾" thick.

Cut into rounds with a 3" fluted cutter.

Place on the baking tray and brush with milk or beaten egg and milk mixture.

Bake near the top of the hot oven for 7 to 10 minutes or until golden brown and well risen.

Cool on a wire rack before eating.

Serve with butter.

Treacle Scones

8 oz self raising flour
2 oz butter
1 oz caster/fine sugar
½ teaspoon of cinnamon
2 tablespoons black treacle (molasses) or golden syrup (light corn syrup)
pinch of salt
¼ pint of milk

Heat the oven to 425F.
Grease and flour a baking sheet, or line with parchment paper.

Sift the flour and salt into a bowl and rub in the butter.

Mix in the sugar, cinnamon, treacle or syrup and enough milk to make a soft dough. Knead this on a floured surface until it is both moist and elastic.

Cut into rounds with a 2.5 inch pastry cutter and place on baking sheet.

Brush with a little milk and bake for 10 - 15 minutes until golden brown.

Allow to cool on a wire rack and serve split in half with butter.

Apple Scones

8 oz self raising flour
2 oz caster/fine sugar
2 teaspoons baking powder
½ teaspoon baking soda
½ teaspoon salt
2 oz butter, chilled
1 apple - peeled, cored and shredded
½ cup milk

<u>For brushing top</u>
2 tablespoons milk for brushing
2 tablespoons sugar
½ teaspoon ground cinnamon

Preheat oven to 425F.
Grease and flour a baking sheet, or line with parchment paper.

Measure flour, sugar, baking powder, baking soda, and salt into a large bowl.

Rub in butter until crumbly. Add shredded apple and milk. Stir to form a soft dough.

Turn dough out onto a lightly floured surface. Knead gently 8 to 10 times.

Pat into two 6-inch circles. Place on greased baking sheet.

Brush tops with milk, and sprinkle with sugar and cinnamon.

Score each into 6 pie-shaped wedges.

Bake for 15 minutes, or until browned and risen.

Serve warm with butter.

Walnut and Raisin Scones

8 oz self raising flour
2 oz caster/fine sugar
2 teaspoons baking powder
½ teaspoon baking soda
½ teaspoon salt
2 oz butter, chilled
1 tablespoon grated lemon zest
¾ cup chopped walnuts
½ cup raisins
¾ cup buttermilk

For brushing top
2 tablespoons buttermilk
2 tablespoons sugar
2 tablespoons chopped walnuts

Preheat oven to 425F.
Grease and flour a baking sheet, or line with parchment paper.

In a large bowl combine flour, sugar, baking powder, baking soda, salt and lemon peel.

Rub in butter. Mix in all but 2 tablespoons of the nuts and the raisins.

Mix in buttermilk with fork.

Gather the dough into a ball and knead for about 2 minutes on lightly floured board. Roll out to ¾ inch thick. With a chef's knife cut into 3 inch triangles.

Place, spaced 1inch apart, on a greased baking sheet.

Brush tops with remaining 1 tablespoon buttermilk; sprinkle with the remaining sugar and the nuts.

Bake in center of oven for about 15 minutes or until nicely browned.

Serve warm with butter or jam.

Cheese Scones

12 oz self raising flour
2 teaspoons baking powder
3 oz butter
11 oz strong grated cheese
6 fl oz milk
1 dash pepper
2 teaspoons mustard powder

Preheat oven to 450F.
Grease and flour a baking sheet, or line with parchment paper.

Sieve the flour and dry ingredients.

Mix in the butter. Add grated cheese, mix well, then add the milk in slowly.

Mix into a dough, pat with hand then cut into shapes. If desired, top with a little grated cheese. Place on baking sheet.

Bake towards top of oven for 7 to 10 minutes until risen with lightly golden tops.

Cool on wire rack.

This sounds weird, but cheese scones are delicious split open and spread with jam.

Potato Scones

8 oz floury potatoes, cut into cubes
8 oz plain flour
1 teaspoon baking powder
2 oz butter, melted, plus extra for frying
3 tablespoons milk
2 eggs, beaten
2 teaspoons oil for frying

Cook the potatoes in plenty of salted simmering water until tender. Drain well and mash.

Sift the flour and baking powder into a bowl, add the butter, milk, eggs, mash and plenty of seasoning and mix to a sticky dough.

Heat some butter and a little oil in a large frying pan. Fry dollops of the mixture for 3 minutes on each side until browned. You may need to do this in 2 batches, so keep the fried ones warm in the oven.

Serve with crisp bacon and grated mature cheddar cheese.

Cheddar and Chive Scones

4 oz extra-sharp cheddar cheese, grated
6 tablespoons minced fresh chives
8 oz plus 1 tablespoon self raising flour
3 large eggs, beaten lightly, plus 1 large egg beaten with 1 tablespoon water for egg wash
½ cup heavy cream
1 tablespoon baking powder
½ teaspoon paprika
1 teaspoon salt
3oz cold unsalted butter, roughly chopped

Preheat oven to 400 degrees.
Cover a baking sheet with a piece of parchment paper.

Place the cheddar cheese, chives, and 1 tablespoon flour in a small bowl, and toss to combine. Set mixture aside.

In a small bowl, combine the 3 lightly beaten eggs and the cream, and set aside.

Combine flour, baking powder, paprika, and salt.

Rub in butter until pea-sized. Add egg-and cream mixture and stir until just blended. Add cheese mixture and mix until just combined.

Transfer dough to a well-floured surface, and pat into a 9-inch circle.

Using a sharp knife dipped in flour, cut circle into 12 wedges. Transfer wedges to prepared baking sheet.

Brush tops with egg wash.

Bake in oven, rotating baking sheet halfway through cooking, until outside is crusty and inside is cooked through, about 15 to 20 minutes.

Transfer to a wire rack to cool.

Soured Cream Scones

8 oz self raising flour
1½ oz cold butter
½ level teaspoon salt
4 tablespoons sour cream
4 tablespoons milk
extra milk for brushing

Heat the oven to 450F.
Grease and flour a baking sheet, or line with parchment paper.

Sift the flour and salt into bowl.

Quickly rub the butter into the flour until the mixture resembles fine breadcrumbs.

Add cream and milk all at once and mix with a knife to a soft but not sticky dough.

Turn the mixture onto a floured board and knead quickly until smooth.

Roll out to about ½ inch thick.

Cut into 9 or 10 rounds.

Place on the baking tray and brush with the beaten egg and milk mixture.

Bake near the top of the hot oven for 7 to 10 minutes until well risen and golden brown.

Cool on a wire rack.

Serve with butter and jam.

Strawberry Yoghurt Scones

8 oz self raising flour
1½ oz cold butter
½ level teaspoon salt
4 tablespoons strawberry (or other flavor) yoghurt
4 tablespoons milk
extra milk for brushing

Heat the oven to 450F.
Grease and flour a baking sheet, or line with parchment paper.

Sift the flour and salt into bowl.

Quickly rub the butter into the flour until the mixture resembles fine breadcrumbs.

Add yoghurt and milk all at once and mix with a knife to a soft but not sticky dough.

Turn the mixture onto a floured board and knead quickly until smooth.

Roll out to about ½ inch thick.

Cut into 9 or 10 rounds.

Place on the baking tray and brush with the beaten egg and milk mixture.

Bake near the top of the hot oven for 7 to 10 minutes until well risen and golden brown.

Cool on a wire rack.

Serve with butter.

Orange and Cherry Scones

8 oz self raising flour
1 level teaspoon baking powder
½ level teaspoon salt
2 oz butter
1 oz caster/fine sugar
½ teaspoon finely grated orange rind
1½ oz finely chopped glace cherries
¼ pint milk
Extra milk for brushing, or egg and milk mixture

Heat oven to 450F.
Grease and flour a baking sheet, or line with parchment paper.

Sift the flour into a roomy baking bowl then add the butter, baking powder and salt.

Quickly rub the butter into the flour until the mixture resembles fine breadcrumbs.

Add sugar, orange rind and cherries and stir.

Make a well in the center and using a dinner knife, stir in enough milk to make a soft, pliable dough.

Turn the mixture onto a floured board and knead very lightly, only 3 or 4 times, until just smooth, then lightly roll out to ¾" thick.

Cut into rounds with a 3" fluted cutter.

Place on the baking tray and brush with milk or beaten egg and milk mixture.

Bake near the top of the hot oven for 7 to 10 minutes or until golden brown and well risen.

Cool on a wire rack before eating.

Serve with butter.

Honey Scones

8 oz self raising flour
1 level teaspoon baking powder
½ level teaspoon salt
2 oz butter
1 oz caster/fine sugar
1 tablespoon warmed honey
7 tablespoons milk
Extra milk for brushing, or egg and milk mixture

Heat oven to 450F.
Grease and flour a baking sheet, or line with parchment paper.

Sift the flour into a roomy baking bowl then add the butter, baking powder and salt.

Quickly rub the butter into the flour until the mixture resembles fine breadcrumbs.

Add sugar and stir.

Make a well in the center and using a dinner knife, stir in milk and honey to make a soft, pliable dough.

Turn the mixture onto a floured board and knead very lightly, only 3 or 4 times, until just smooth, then lightly roll out to ¾" thick.

Cut into rounds with a 3" fluted cutter.

Place on the baking tray and brush with milk or beaten egg and milk mixture.

Bake near the top of the hot oven for 7 to 10 minutes or until golden brown and well risen.

Cool on a wire rack before eating.

Serve with butter.

Dropped Scones

8 oz self raising flour
½ level teaspoon salt
1 level teaspoon caster/fine sugar
1 medium egg
½ pint milk
1 to 2 oz melted butter

Sift flour and salt into a bowl.

Add sugar, egg and half the milk and mix to a smooth creamy batter.

Stir in the rest of the milk.

Brush large heavy frying pan with melted butter and heat.

Using a spoon, drop (about 12) small rounds of scone mixture into pan.

Cook until bubbles show on surface, about 2½ to 3 minutes.

Carefully turn over with a knife and cool for another 2 minutes.

Pile scones into clean, folded tea towel to keep warm.

Serve immediately with butter and jam, or honey.

Section 4. Biscuits

Biscuits. Another great British tradition. Put the kettle on, brew a pot of tea and settle down with a good plate of bickies. Now that I live in America I've had to get used to calling them cookies. Biscuits here look more like English scones. Delicious, but you can't dunk them in your tea or coffee like you can real biscuits.

I thought it would be great to put together a book of all the traditional British biscuit recipes I could lay my hands on. Of course, not many people make their own these days, especially as there are so many wonderful varieties to be found in the supermarket. But they really are so easy to make and so yummy. Great fun to do with the kids on a rainy day.

Digestives

I had to start with this most well-known of British biscuits. Commercial varieties of these can be found throughout the world. Sometimes known as wheatmeal biscuits and often covered in chocolate to make them extra "naughty but nice".

4 oz. fine or medium oatmeal
1½ oz fine sugar
4 oz wholewheat flour
3 oz butter
A pinch of salt
A small pinch of bicarbonate of soda
½ egg, beaten (? you have to break it open first!)

Preheat oven to 375F. Grease a baking sheet.

Rub butter into flour and oatmeal, add sugar, salt and bicarbonate of soda.

Bind with the beaten egg, put the dough on pastry-board sprinkled with oatmeal, and roll out.

Sprinkle lightly with oatmeal, roll it in, and then cut with 3" cookie cutter.

Bake for about 12 to 14 minutes.

Gingernuts

No nuts to be found in these classic biscuits. Why the name? No clue! I hated these as a child as I found them too spicy. My sister on the other hand loved them.

4 oz self raising flour
1 level teaspoon ground ginger
¼ level teaspoon mixed spice
2 oz butter
1½ oz brown or fine sugar
1 level tablespoon melted black treacle or blackstrap molasses
milk to mix

Preheat oven to 350F. Grease baking sheet.

Sift flour, ginger and spice into a bowl and rub in the butter.

Add sugar and mix to a very stiff paste with treacle and milk.

Roll out very thinly and cut into 26 to 30 rounds with a 2 inch cutter.

Bake just above the center for 10 minutes.
Cool on the baking sheet for a few minutes then, using a palette knife, remove to a wire rack to cool completely.

Flapjacks

Nothing like the American flapjacks which are pancakes, these oaty biscuits are a good old British staple and can often be found in railway station cafes. They could be used as door stops if you over-bake them!

4 oz butter
3 oz golden syrup or light corn syrup or molasses
3 oz soft brown sugar
8 oz rolled oats

Preheat oven to 350F.
Line a baking sheet with parchment.

Put butter, syrup and sugar into a pan and melt over a low heat.

Stir in oats and mix well.

Spread into baking sheet and bake in center of oven for 30 minutes or less if you like them more chewy.

Leave in sheet for 5 minutes then cut into fingers.

Remove from sheet when cold.

Shrewsbury Biscuits

Light, lemony biscuits which will stay fresh for up to a week if stored in an airtight container.

Makes about 18 biscuits.

4 oz butter, softened, plus a little more for greasing
6 oz fine sugar, plus a little more for sprinkling
2 egg yolks, plus 1 egg white
8 oz plain flour, sifted
½ teaspoon caraway seeds
Finely grated zest of 1 lemon
Pinch of salt
1-2 tablespoons whole milk

Preheat oven to 350F.
Line two baking sheets with baking parchment.

In a large bowl, cream the butter and sugar until pale and fluffy. Beat in the egg yolks one at a time.

Fold in the flour, caraway, zest, salt and just enough milk to bring it together into a smooth dough – you may not need the milk at all, depending on the size of the egg yolks.

Turn out the dough on to a lightly floured surface and knead gently into a disc. Roll out to about ¼ to ⅛ inch thick.
Cut out biscuits with a 2½ inch plain or fluted cutter.

Arrange on the sheets and bake for 10 minutes.

While they are cooking, lightly beat the egg white.

Remove the biscuits from the oven, brush lightly with egg white and sprinkle with caster sugar, then bake for four or five minutes more, until pale golden brown around the edges.

Cool on the sheet, then transfer to wire racks to cool completely.

Ayrshire Shortbread

4 oz ground rice
4 oz flour
4 oz butter
4 oz fine sugar
1 egg yolk, beaten
1 tablespoon double cream
1 drop vanilla essence

Preheat oven to 350F. Grease a baking sheet.

Sift the flour and ground rice into a bowl.

Rub in the butter and add the sugar.

Add the beaten egg yolk, cream and vanilla and mix.

Knead well on a floured board until stiff. Do not add any extra moisture.

Roll out thinly. Prick with a fork and cut into fingers.

Place on baking sheet and bake for 15 to 20 minutes until golden brown.

Almond Shortbread

6 oz flour
2 oz cornflour
5 oz butter
1 oz ground almonds
3 oz fine sugar

Preheat oven to 350F. Grease a baking sheet.

Cream the butter in a mixing bowl.

Sift together the flour and cornflour and add with the almonds and sugar to the butter.

Work the ingredients together with your hands.

Turn out onto a very lightly floured surface and knead until smooth.

Roll dough into 2 rounds each about ¼ inch thick. Prick well with fork and mark each circle into 6 triangles.

Transfer to baking sheet and bake for 25 to 30 minutes.

Allow to cool slightly before cutting and then place on a wire cooling rack.

Petticoat Tails

4 oz butter, softened
2 oz fine sugar, plus extra for top
5 oz flour
2 oz ground rice

Preheat oven to 325F.

Cream the butter and sugar together until pale and fluffy.

Gradually stir in the flour and ground rice. Draw the mixture together and press into a 7 inch round shallow cake pan.

Prick well all over with a fork and pinch up the edges with a finger and thumb or the edge of a spoon.

Mark into 8 triangles with a sharp knife.

Bake for about 40 minutes, until pale straw in color.

Leave in the tin for 5 minutes, cut into 8 triangles, then dredge with caster sugar.

Remove from the tin when cold. Store in an airtight container.

Garibaldi Biscuits

The Garibaldi biscuit is basically a currant sandwich. It consists of currants squashed between two thin oblongs of biscuit. It was named after an Italian general during the mid 18oo's.

2 oz chopped currants
2 tablespoons milk
1 oz butter
4 oz self raising flour
pinch of salt
1 oz fine sugar

Preheat oven to 375F. Grease a baking sheet.

Sift all the dry ingredients together into a bowl
Add the milk and butter and mix firmly into a smooth dough using a fork.

Turn onto a well floured board, roll out to about an eighth of an inch thick and cut down the center.

Spread the chopped currants on one half of the dough and cover with the other half.

Roll again to press together and cut into rectangles.

Brush lightly with water and sprinkle with the sugar.

Bake for about 15 minutes.

Cornish Fairings

4 oz butter, softened
4 oz fine sugar
2 tablespoons golden syrup or light corn syrup
7 oz self raising flour
1 teaspoon ground ginger
¼-½ teaspoon ground mixed spice (U.S. allspice)
¼ teaspoon ground cinnamon
¼ teaspoon bicarbonate of soda
Pinch of salt

Preheat oven to 400F.
Line two baking sheets with baking parchment.

Melt the butter, sugar and golden syrup in a pan over a low heat. Remove from heat and stir well.

Sift the flour, ginger, mixed spice, cinnamon, bicarbonate of soda and salt together into a bowl.

Add flour etc to the melted butter mixture and gently beat to form a smooth dough.

Roll the still-warm dough into balls the size of a small walnut and place 1 inch apart on the prepared sheets.

Bake for 10 minutes, remove from the oven and carefully bash the sheets on the counter to make the biscuits crackle and spread.

Return to the oven for five to seven minutes, until golden brown.

Cool on the sheets for a few minutes, then transfer to a wire rack to cool completely.

Abernethy Biscuits

Dr John Abernethy, surgeon at St Bart's in London, who either invented himself or had named for him the "Abernethy biscuit". Apparently an indifferent surgeon but an excellent lecturer, he was a dogmatic and curmudgeonly man who believed that most diseases were due to disordered digestion.

8 oz flour
½ teaspoon baking powder
3 oz butter
3 oz fine sugar
1 beaten egg
1 tablespoon milk
½ teaspoon caraway seeds (optional)

Preheat oven to 350F. Grease a baking sheet.

Sift the flour and baking powder into a bowl.

Rub in the butter well until it resembles fine breadcrumbs.

Add the sugar and caraway seeds if desired.

Add the beaten egg and the milk and mix thoroughly until it forms a sticky dough.

Roll out thinly on a floured surface. Cut into rounds with a 2 inch cutter.

Place on baking sheet and cook for 10 to 15 minutes until pale gold in color.

Jam Thumb Biscuits

Very easy to make. Even if you've never made biscuits before you will not go wrong with these.

5 oz unsalted butter at room temperature
5 oz fine or vanilla sugar
Finely grated zest of 1 lemon
½ tsp vanilla extract
2 egg yolks
2 tablespoons milk
10 oz flour, sifted with a good pinch of salt
About 6 tablespoons jam

Preheat oven 350F. Line 2 baking sheets with parchment.

Beat the butter and sugar in a large bowl until light and fluffy, then beat in the lemon zest and vanilla extract.

Beat in the egg yolks one at a time, then beat in the milk.

Gently fold in half the flour, stir gently, then add the rest – don't overwork it or the biscuits will be tough.

Pull together gently with your hands until you have a smooth ball. Wrap in plastic, chill for 30 minutes, then roll into 1 inch balls. Place these on the baking sheets about 1 inch apart.

Dip your thumb in water and push a deep well in the centre of each ball.

Put a teaspoon or two of jam in each indentation.

Bake for about 15 minutes until firm to touch and golden on the bottom.

Leave to cool on the sheet for a few minutes, then transfer to wire racks and cool completely.

Bourbon Biscuits

Pronounced "bore-bon" and made with chocolate not bourbon. Although I guess you could add some if you wished! A sandwich biscuit made of two thin oblong chocolate biscuits with a chocolate fondant filling. They are particularly yummy dunked into a milky mug of coffee or Ovaltine.

4 oz flour
1 oz butter
2 oz sugar
½ teaspoon baking soda
½ teaspoon baking powder
1 tablespoon cocoa/chocolate powder
¾ teaspoon vanilla
1½ teaspoons honey
3-4 tablespoons milk

Filling
1 oz butter
1 oz confectioners' sugar
1 teaspoon cocoa
1 teaspoon vanilla

Preheat oven to 325F. Grease a baking sheet.

Sieve flour, baking soda, baking powder and cocoa together. In another bowl, mix butter, sugar, vanilla essence and honey together.

Mix in the dry ingredients and add milk a little by little to make a soft dough.

Roll out on lightly floured surface.

Cut the rolled dough in to equal sized rectangles.

Sprinkle sugar on the top and prick holes with a fork in 3 places at equal distances.

Bake for 15 minutes. Cool for couple of minutes.

Spread filling onto one side of one biscuit and then place another on top and press down gently.

Custard Creams

6 oz flour
2 oz (Bird's) custard powder OR 2 oz cornstarch and 1 teaspoon vanilla extract
¼ teaspoon baking soda
2 oz confectioners' sugar
6 oz butter, softened
a few drops vanilla extract

<u>Cream filling</u>
2 oz confectioners' sugar
1 oz butter, softened
2 tablespoons custard powder OR 2 tablespoons cornstarch and ½ teaspoon vanilla extract

Preheat oven to 325F. Line a baking sheet with parchment paper.

Cream sugar with butter until fluffy. Add vanilla extract.

Sift the flour with the baking soda, and custard powder, or cornstarch.

Add dry mixture to the creamed mix and combine well.

Roll into small balls and flatten with the back of a fork.
Bake about 8 minutes until bottoms are just turning golden.

Remove to cooling rack and cool completely.

<u>Cream filling</u>

Combine sugar with butter and custard powder/corn starch until creamy and spreadable.

Spread on the bottom of one biscuit and top with the bottom of another, to make a sandwich.

Anzac Biscuits

Australians have claimed these chewy treats as they were made during WW1 by mothers, wives and girlfriends and shipped to soldiers serving at the front. However, the original recipe can be traced back to Scotland.

3 oz medium oatmeal
3 oz desiccated coconut
4 oz flour
4 oz fine sugar
4 oz butter, melted
1 tablespoon golden syrup or light corn syrup or molasses
1 teaspoon bicarbonate of soda

Preheat the oven 350F. Grease a baking sheet.

Put the oats, coconut, flour and sugar in a bowl.

Melt the butter in a small pan, or microwave and stir in the golden syrup.

Add the bicarbonate of soda to 2 tablespoons of boiling water, then stir into the golden syrup and butter mixture.

Make a well in the center of the dry ingredients and pour in the liquid. Stir gently to incorporate the dry ingredients.

Put dessertspoonfuls of the mixture onto baking sheet about 1 inch apart to allow room for spreading.

Bake in batches for 8-10 minutes until golden.
Transfer to a wire rack to cool.

Treacle Bites

Similar to Anzac biscuits.

4 oz self raising flour
3 oz rolled oats
1 oz dessicated coconut
4 oz butter
5 oz fine sugar
2 tablespoons treacle or blackstrap molasses
1 level teaspoon bicarbonate of soda dissolved in 1 tablespoon milk.

Grease a baking sheet.

Combine flour with oats and coconut.

Put butter, sugar and treacle into saucepan. Gently bring to a boil stirring all the time.

Remove from heat. Add bicarbonate and milk mix.
Pour hot liquid into dry ingredients and mix thoroughly.

Leave for 30 minutes until firm.

Preheat oven to 350F.

Break off 24 pieces of mixture and roll into marble sized balls.

Transfer to baking sheet leaving room between each for spreading.

Bake in center of oven for 15 minutes.
Leave on sheet for 2 minutes and then cool on wire rack.

Rich Tea Biscuits

A plain, round biscuit, originally called Tea Biscuits, they were developed in the 17th century in Yorkshire for the upper-classes as a light snack between full-course meals. Rich tea biscuits are sweet and slightly crisp and perfectly accompany a cup of tea. Like biscotti for coffee, the rich tea biscuit is meant for dunking, but unlike biscotti, one dunk is the maximum as the rich tea biscuit crumbles easily when wet.

Preheat oven to 375F. Grease a baking sheet.

2 tablespoons golden syrup
3 oz butter or canola oil
8 oz self raising flour
pinch of salt
1 egg

Warm the syrup and beat to a cream with the butter. Gradually beat in the flour and salt, with the egg to make a stiff mixture.

Knead lightly on a floured board, roll out thinly, prick all over with a fork or skewer and cut into 3 inch rounds.

Bake about 12 minutes until crisp and lightly browned.
Cool on baking sheet then remove to a wire tray.

Savory Cheesy Biscuits

6 oz flour
½ teaspoon mustard powder
2 oz unsalted butter
2 oz Stilton or blue cheese
2 oz grated strong cheddar cheese
6 oz crunchy peanut butter
1 egg, beaten

Preheat oven to 400F.

Place flour and mustard in a bowl.

Add butter and rub in until the mixture resembles fine breadcrumbs.

Stir in cheeses, and then add the peanut butter and egg and mix well.

Roll out on a floured work surface to ¼ inch thick, cut out with a 2 inch biscuit cutter or into assorted shapes.

Place on dry baking sheets and bake for 10-15 minutes.

Cool on a wire rack. Serve warm or cold.

Coffee Biscuits

Extremely easy to make and perfect with a cup of tea or coffee.

1 tablespoon treacle
1 tablespoon sugar
2 tablespoons butter
1 teaspoon mixed spice
pinch of salt
2 tablespoons black coffee
1 level teaspoon baking soda
wheat flour to mix

Preheat oven to 375F. Grease a baking sheet.

Put ingredients, except soda and flour, into saucepan and stir over a gentle heat until dissolved.

Cool slightly, then stir in the soda and enough flour to make a firm dough.

Knead, roll out to about ¼ inch thick, and cut into rounds.

Bake for 15 to 20 minutes.

Arrowroot Biscuits

A very plain, semi-sweet biscuit.

4 oz self raising flour
2 oz arrowroot
1 level tablespoon sugar
2 oz butter
1 egg
squeeze of lemon juice
milk if necessary

Preheat oven to 300F. Grease baking sheet.

Mix the dry ingredients and rub in butter.

Mix to a stiff paste with the egg and lemon juice, adding milk only if required.

Roll out very thin on a floured board, prick with a fork and cut into rounds with a fluted cutter.

Bake for about 20 minutes until golden brown.

Jammie Dodgers

British kids love these. I guess they are the Brit equivalent of Oreos. The texture is somewhat like shortbread, with seedless raspberry jam sandwiched between. One side of the cookie is cut out in the middle in a heart or round shape.

4 oz butter
4 oz fine sugar
4 oz flour
1 oz cornstarch
seedless raspberry jam

Preheat oven to 350F. Grease a baking sheet.

Cream the butter and sugar together until pale and fluffy, then stir in flour and cornstarch to form a dough, adding more flour if necessary.

Chill the dough wrapped in plastic for 20 minutes, then roll out to about ¼ inch thick between two sheets of cling wrap or waxed paper.

Cut out 12 rounds about 2½ inch and cut a smaller heart shape or circle in the centre, about an inch in size. Re-roll dough if needed using the scraps to make 12 more 2½ inch rounds.

Bake for 8-10 minutes, then cool on a wire rack.

Sandwich together with jam and sprinkle with powdered sugar if desired.

Crumpets

8 oz strong plain flour
1 level teaspoon salt
1 level tablespoon dried yeast
1 level teaspoon caster sugar
½ pint (275 ml) milk
2 fl oz (55 ml) water
You will also need a thick-based frying pan or griddle, 3inch cooking rings and a little oil.

Heat the milk and water together in a small saucepan till they are 'hand hot'. Then pour into a jug, stir in the sugar and dried yeast and leave it in a warm place for 10-15 minutes till there is a good frothy head on it.

Meanwhile, sift the flour and salt into a mixing bowl and make a well in the centre. When the yeast mixture is frothy, pour it all into the mixing bowl.

Slowly work the flour into the liquid with a wooden spoon. Beat well at the end to make a perfectly smooth batter.

Cover the mixing bowl with a tea-towel and leave to stand in a warm place for about 45 minutes, by which time, the batter will have become light and frothy.

When you're ready to cook, grease the insides of the cooking rings very well and add a little oil to your frying pan before placing it over a medium heat.

When the pan is hot, arrange the rings in the frying pan and spoon 1 tablespoon of the batter into each ring.

Let them cook for 4 or 5 minutes: first tiny bubbles will appear on the surface and then, suddenly, they will burst, leaving the traditional holes.

Now take a large spoon and fork, lift off the rings and turn the crumpets over. Cook on the second side for about 1 minute only.

Re-grease and reheat the rings and pan before cooking the next batch.

Serve the crumpets while still warm, generously buttered and topped with anything that takes your fancy. Strawberry jam or lemon curd are particularly good.

If you are making your teatime treat in advance, then reheat them by toasting lightly on both sides before serving. (Bought crumpets need toasting on the highest setting of your toaster to give you a similar result.)

If you have enjoyed this book and recipes I would greatly appreciate it if you could take a few minutes and post a review.

http://www.amazon.com/Traditional-British-Recipes-Collection-ebook/dp/B00885YZ2I

Printed in Great Britain
by Amazon